I0570305

PRAISE TO THE LORD, THE ALMIGHTY

Praise to the Lord, the Almighty

Gwendolyn Harmon

Contents

Copyright © 2024 by Gwendolyn Harmon
All rights reserved. No part of this book may be reproduced in any manner whatsoever without written permission except in the case of brief quotations embodied in critical articles and reviews.
First Printing, 2024

To my aunt and uncle, who love the old hymns.

Praise to the Lord, the Almighty

by Joachim Neander
(Translated by Catherine Winkworth)

Praise to the Lord, the Almighty, the King of creation!
O my soul, praise Him, for He is thy health and salvation!
All ye who hear, now to His temple draw near;
Praise Him in glad adoration.

Praise to the Lord, who o'er all things so wondrously reigneth,
Shelters thee under His wings, yea, so gently sustaineth!
Hast thou not seen how thy desires e'er have been
Granted in what He ordaineth?

Praise to the Lord, who doth prosper thy work and defend thee;
Surely His goodness and mercy here daily attend thee;
Ponder anew what the Almighty can do,
If with His love He befriend thee.

Praise to the Lord, who, when tempests their warfare are waging,
Who, when the elements madly around thee are raging,
Biddeth them cease, turneth their fury to peace,
Whirlwinds and waters assuaging.

Praise to the Lord, who, when darkness of sin is abounding,
Who, when the godless do triumph, all virtue confounding,
Sheddeth His light, chaseth the horrors of night,
Saints with His mercy surrounding.

Praise to the Lord, O let all that is in me adore Him!
All that hath life and breath, come now with praises before Him;
Let the Amen sound from His people again,
Gladly for aye we adore Him.

1

Praise to the Lord

PRAISE TO THE LORD, THE ALMIGHTY, THE KING OF CREATION

"Praise the Lord!" It's a phrase we hear often. In fact, you might have heard, said, or sung this phrase more than once within the last 24 hours. But whether you're a brand-new believer or one who has walked with the Lord a long time, we would all do well to stop now and then and consider Who it is we are praising.

This word, *Lord*, is found many times throughout the Bible. It is the Hebrew name God uses for Himself in Exodus 3:14:

"And God said unto Moses, I AM THAT I AM: and He said, Thus shalt thou say unto the children of Israel, I AM hath sent me unto you."

God's use of that phrase, "I Am," is really the declaration of His self-existence and self-sufficiency. When we say or sing, "Praise the

Lord," we are praising the God who needs nothing, is dependent upon nothing—and upon Whom we depend for everything.

You may be familiar with Paul's message on Mars hill, where he addressed a crowd of pagan worshipers who had built an altar to worship the God they did not know.

"For as I passed by, and beheld your devotions, I found an altar with this inscription, TO THE UNKNOWN GOD. Whom therefore ye ignorantly worship, Him declare I unto you. God that made the world and all things therein, seeing that He is Lord of heaven and earth, dwelleth not in temples made with hands; Neither is worshipped with men's hands, as though He needed any thing, seeing He giveth to all life, and breath, and all things;"(Acts 17:23-25)

All that we have, down to our very existence itself, the very air we breathe—all of it comes from and is dependent upon God, Who in turn needs nothing from us, but lovingly, graciously accepts our humble (and wholly inadequate) offerings of praise.

What aspect of the self-existence or self-sufficiency of God is the Holy Spirit bringing to your attention today? Remember to praise Him for it!

2

The Almighty

PRAISE TO THE LORD, THE ALMIGHTY...

The word *almighty* is one of those easy words that mean precisely what they say. Our God is worthy to be praised, because He is *all-mighty*—he has all might, all power. Theologians call this omnipotence, and it is an attribute which only God possesses.

You probably know in your head that God is almighty, but sometimes we act as if the omnipotence of God is just a nice theory, instead of a certain truth. The prophet Jeremiah was brought face to face with the difference between mere knowledge and true belief in the omnipotence of God in Jeremiah 32.

God told him to go buy a certain field, but had already told Jeremiah that the enemy was about to utterly destroy the city and take its people captive, removing them to a far-off land. Jeremiah vented his confusion to God, but prefaced it with this statement:

"Ah, Lord God! Behold, thou hast made the heaven and the earth by Thy great power and stretched out arm, and there is nothing too hard for Thee" (32:17)

He *knew* there was nothing too hard for God, but couldn't quite figure out why God would want him to waste his money paying for a field that would soon be property of an enemy nation.

But God replied to Jeremiah with a question that brought him back to the heart of the matter:

"Behold, I am the Lord, the God of all flesh: is there any thing too hard for Me?" (32:27)

God took Jeremiah back to his own words. There is indeed *nothing* too hard for God, but Jeremiah was thinking of his infinite God on finite terms. He needed his faith brought back into focus on Who his God really was.

God then graciously gave Jeremiah a fuller view of His plan, promising the return of His people to the land He had given them. The very act Jeremiah saw as futile, God intended as a symbol of the certainty of His faithfulness—and His power to perform what He had promised.

Has any finite thinking crept between you and the Almighty God you serve today?

3

The King of Creation

PRAISE TO THE LORD, THE ALMIGHTY, THE KING OF CREATION

The Bible begins with the truth of God's right to reign over His creation. Consider the grand, yet simple statement of the very first verse of the Bible:

"In the beginning God created the heaven and the earth." (Genesis 1:1)

As Creator, God is worthy of our worship and devotion. As we have already seen, we are dependent upon Him for everything. Nehemiah 9:6 puts it this way,

"Thou, even Thou, art Lord alone; Thou hast made heaven, the heaven of heavens, with all their host, the earth, and all things that are therein, the seas, and all that is therein, and Thou preservest them all; and the host of heaven worshippeth Thee."

Isaiah also touches on God's status as Lord over all creation:

"O Lord of hosts, God of Israel, that dwellest between the cherubims, Thou art the God, even Thou alone, of all the kingdoms of the earth: Thou hast made heaven and earth."(37:16)

The point is, our God is the King of Creation, and He alone is worthy of worship.

"Thou art worthy, O Lord, to receive glory and honour and power: for Thou hast created all things, and for Thy pleasure they are and were created. (Revelation 4:11)

So what does that mean for us today? There are two practical applications that come to mind: first, that God reigns over His creation. He is sovereign and in control, and we can trust Him with every facet and detail of our lives.

The second practical way this truth applies to our lives is that God alone is worthy of our worship—but we often let other things become more important to us.

How important is God to you today?
Have you taken time to worship Him, praying and reading His
Word, or are other things crowding Him out?

4

My Health

O MY SOUL, PRAISE HIM FOR HE IS THY HEALTH AND SALVATION

Psalm 42 is the cry of a heart surrounded by trouble. The psalmist thirsts for God, but feels separated from Him by the heavy load of false accusations and derision. He is overwhelmed by emotion, and yet, as the psalmist acknowledges his feelings of despair, loneliness, and affliction, he remembers the crucial thing:

"Yet the Lord will command His lovingkindness in the daytime, and in the night His song shall be with me, and my prayer unto the God of my life." *(Psalm 4:8)*

His situation had not changed, his emotions may still have been in turmoil, but the psalmist chose to remember God, and to cling to the truth that God's lovingkindness does not fail—to the truth that, although all the world seemed to have forsaken him, God never would.

Our spiritual health (along with our physical health) depends on God. When we are close to Him, no matter what is happening in our lives or the lives of those around us, we can rest in the certainty of His presence and His promises.

As the songwriter points out, He is our health. The psalmist points this out as well:

"Why art thou cast down, O my soul? and why art thou disquieted within me? hope thou in God: for I shall yet praise Him, Who is the health of my countenance, and my God." Psalm v.11

Are you feeling overwhelmed or far from God today? Heed the psalmist's words and *"hope thou in God."* Choose to praise Him and to remember the unchanging truths of Who He is.

How is the Holy Spirit calling you to draw near to Him today?

5

My Salvation

O MY SOUL, PRAISE HIM, FOR HE IS THY HEALTH AND SALVATION

One benefit of working with children is the joy of being reminded of simple truths. Every year, I am reminded just how much we take for granted that which is familiar or basic. But we need those simple truths now just as much as we did the day we trusted Christ for salvation. Consider John 3:16, for example:

"For God so loved the world, that He gave His only begotten Son, that whosoever believeth in Him should not perish, but have everlasting life."

We have a tendency to skim over familiar verses like this, but however familiar it is, it should never become stale to us. God loved the world. He loved it so much that He gave His Son, not just a Son, but His *only* Son, for the sole purpose of making a way for each individual sinner to be saved from hell.

The love of God on display in the finished work of the cross is staggering—but often overlooked by all but the newest Christians.

Yet, we know that in heaven we will still be praising God for His saving work. Revelation 19:1 tells us,

"And after these things I heard a great voice of much people in heaven, saying, Alleluia; Salvation, and glory, and honour, and power, unto the Lord our God."

When was the last time you really *thought* about your salvation? The church in Ephesus was told to return to their "first love" in their relationship with Christ by doing two simple things:

"Remember therefore from whence thou art fallen, and repent, and do the first works" (Revelation 2:5a)

Take time to consider the love and mercy of your Savior. What actions does God want the joy of your salvation to inspire in your life today?

6

Drawing Near

ALL YE WHO HEAR, NOW TO HIS TEMPLE DRAW NEAR

The purpose of this little book is to help you draw near to the Lord. While we do not have a physical temple to worship at, our hearts can still draw near to God. In fact, we have a personal and precious invitation to the very throne room of God:

"Having therefore, brethren, boldness to enter into the holiest by the blood of Jesus, By a new and living way, which He hath consecrated for us, through the veil, that is to say, His flesh; And having an High Priest over the house of God; Let us draw near with a true heart in full assurance of faith, having our hearts sprinkled from an evil conscience, and our bodies washed with pure water." (Hebrews 10:19-22)

As those who served God in the earthly temple, we must be made pure, cleansed from sin. We are made pure by the blood of Christ, and thus can go before the Lord any time we want, to pray, yes—but also to praise Him.

It is no accident that this passage about drawing near to Christ personally continues on to give us a very clear command regarding drawing near corporately:

"And let us consider one another to provoke unto love and to good works: Not forsaking the assembling of ourselves together, as the manner of some is; but exhorting one another: and so much the more, as ye see the day approaching." (Hebrews 10:24-25)

The Christian life requires personal *and* corporate nearness to God. He has designed us to be close to Him individually, so that He can use us to spur each other on toward greater Christlikeness.

And how do we get close to God? James 4:8 gives us a command, along with an inexpressibly precious truth:

"Draw nigh to God, and He will draw nigh to you..." James 4:8

As we draw nigh, He is active in promoting our closeness of fellowship with Him. Our loving God meets our seeking, searching, stumbling hearts with the unfailing nearness of His grace. He draws us ever closer as we simply take time in His presence throughout each day, deepening and developing our relationship with Him.

Think about your walk with God: are you close to Him?
Does your closeness help others draw nearer to Him?

7

Glad Adoration

JOIN ME IN GLAD ADORATION!

When it is time to meet with God, either corporately or in private, are you *glad* for the opportunity? Modern Christianity has all but lost the sense of wonder and awe at Who God is, to the extent that attending church or making time for personal worship has become something we often look on as mere duty, just one more thing to fit into our schedule.

But that is not the Biblical pattern. We should be eager for our times with God, and worship should flow from hearts filled to overflowing with wonder, awe, and gratitude for all He is and does. The psalmist said,

"I was glad when they said unto me, Let us go into the house of the Lord."(Psalm 122:1)

So what makes the difference? How do we become "glad" to worship God? Before you go to worship, whether at home by yourself or on the way to church, think about Who it is you are about to worship.

Think about how God has shown His power, mercy, goodness, and strength in your own life. Let yourself get excited about the God who loves you enough to die for your sins, and who is powerful enough to raise Himself from the dead in triumph over sin and death.

Think of His greatness, and rejoice in His unchangeableness. Read passages like Psalm 34, and ponder the many facets of our flawless God.

Are you glad for the opportunity to worship your great God? What is the Holy Spirit calling you to rejoice in most as you worship Him today?

8

Who Wondrously Reigneth

PRAISE TO THE LORD, WHO O'ER ALL THINGS SO WONDROUSLY REIGNETH

Let's stop to ponder this King of Kings whom we worship. Perhaps, living in the United States, the concept of a king and kingdom seem far off from our everyday lives, but the sovereignty of God is a source of great encouragement, just waiting for us to remember it.

The Bible is full of references to God's sovereign reign over his creation. But when was the last time you (or I, for that matter,) stopped to praise God for reigning over all things? Psalm 97:1 reminds us that God's sovereignty is reason for rejoicing!

"The Lord reigneth; let the earth rejoice; let the multitude of isles be glad thereof."

I think we often lose sight of the wonder and majesty of our sovereign God, because it sometimes feels like He *isn't* reigning. Psalm 73 tells of a time when the psalmist was dismayed at the seeming prosperity of the wicked, but notice what pulls him out of his discouragement:

"When I thought to know this, it was too painful for me; Until I went into the sanctuary of God; then understood I their end." (vv.16-7)

When it appears that the wicked are unchecked, unhindered, and thriving, we must remember that our sovereign God is just. His timing may not match ours—He is more merciful than we are, and often allows even the most blatant sinners a season of longsuffering in order to give time for repentance. But that is encouraging as well, because we can trust that His timing is perfect, and we can rejoice that our King of Kings is both just and merciful.

What aspect of God's sovereign reign is the Holy Spirit drawing your attention to today?

9

Gently Sustaining

SHELTERS THEE UNDER HIS WINGS, YEA, SO GENTLY SUSTAINETH!

"I laid me down and slept, I awaked; for the Lord sustained me." Psalm 3:5

Each morning, we wake from sleep because God has sustained us. He is not only the source of life itself, but of the air we breath, the food we eat, the water we drink. He provides us with our physical shelter as well as the comfort of His presence. Psalm 91 describes this beautifully:

"He that dwelleth in the secret place of the most High shall abide under the shadow of the Almighty. I will say of the Lord, He is my refuge and my fortress: my God; in Him will I trust." (vv.1-2)

We are every moment sustained by God. He Himself is our refuge, our source of both safety and strength. Just as the sovereignty of God is a comfort to us in trials, the omnipotence of God is a comfort when we feel that our enemies are just too strong. Whatever opposition God allows in our lives, we can rest in the certainty that He is stronger and greater. He is not only undefeated, but *undefeatable*. As Jesus said,

"These things have I spoken unto you, that in Me ye might have peace. In the world ye shall have tribulation: but be of good cheer, I have overcome the world." John 16:33

The sustenance of God can never be depleted; it will never run out. But while we praise Him for His sustaining power in our lives, we can also praise Him for the wisdom He exercises in sustaining us. James 1:17 says,

"Every good gift and every perfect gift is from above, and cometh down from the Father of lights, with Whom is no variableness, neither shadow of turning."

What are you facing today? What enemies feel too strong for you?
What needs seem too great for God to provide?
Run to God, trusting Him to shelter and sustain you.

10

Desires Granted

HAST THOU NOT SEEN HOW THY DESIRES E'ER HAVE BEEN GRANTED IN WHAT HE ORDAINETH?

Another amazing attribute of our God is that He delights in answering our prayers. As the hymn writer points out, you can probably look back on your life and see many times when God has granted the thing you desired, answering your prayer with a "yes."

When we pray, we can ask God for the desires of our heart in confidence, knowing that He will give all that is according to His will. But notice that even the verse above does not give a blanket promise that God will do every single thing we ask. It is *"the desire of the righteous"* that will be granted, and as James 4:2 points out,

"Ye lust, and have not: ye kill, and desire to have, and cannot obtain: ye fight and war, yet ye have not, because ye ask not. Ye ask, and receive not, because ye ask amiss, that ye may consume it upon your lusts."

God makes no promise to fulfill the sinful desires of our hearts. But when you and I are walking in the Spirit, our hearts will naturally desire that which pleases God, that which is in His will. Then, we can rejoice as we see Psalm 37:4 in action:

"Delight thyself also in the Lord; and He shall give thee the desires of thine heart."

As we delight in the Lord, He changes our hearts, and gives us new desires—desires that align with His will. Truly, He grants our desires in "what He ordaineth."

How is it with your desires today?
Are they the result of delighting in the Lord?

11

Prospering and Defending

"PRAISE TO THE LORD, WHO DOTH PROSPER THY WORK AND DEFEND THEE"

"*But let all those that put their trust in Thee rejoice: let them ever shout for joy, because Thou defendest them; let them also that love Thy name be joyful in Thee. For Thou, Lord, wilt bless the righteous; with favour wilt Thou compass him as with a shield.*" Psalm 5:11-12

I tend to take God's help and defense for granted. I get up, drive to work or church, go about my daily life, and return home to sleep peacefully till morning—all without a single thought for the fact that God kept me safe while I slept, watched over me as I traveled, helped me accomplish my daily tasks, and was there with me every moment to protect and enable me to do all I needed to do. And even though I so often don't remember to thank Him for protecting and prospering me, He does it anyway!

This is yet another reason we have to praise God. Throughout the book of Psalms we see God described as our Strength, our Shield, our

Fortress and Defender. God is all this and more, but we cannot expect God to defend us on our own terms.

As Elsabeth Elliott famously said, "God will not protect you from anything that will make you more like Jesus."

In those times in our lives when it seems that God is closing a door, or has allowed something that seems to us a lapse in His defense, we can lean into Him, and trust that He in His wisdom has allowed that very thing for the purpose of making us more like Him.

Paul wrote in the midst of his imprisonment, *"But I would ye should understand, brethren, that the things which happened unto me have fallen out rather unto the furtherance of the gospel." (Philippians 1:12)*

Although God allowed Paul to be falsely accused and imprisoned, He also used those very things to open doors of opportunity for the gospel. God could have supernaturally protected Paul, but He had a purpose for what Paul was going to go through.

As we praise the Lord for His defending and prospering our acts of obedience to His will, we can also praise Him for His trustworthiness. He is a Defender who can never fail us! Whether or not we see His purpose now, we can trust that He knows what He is doing.

**What is the Holy Spirit teaching you
about your Defender today?**

12

Goodness and Mercy

SURELY HIS GOODNESS AND MERCY HERE DAILY ATTEND THEE;

Among the inexhaustible attributes of God, His mercy and goodness stand together as a reminder of the perfect completeness of God. He is wholly, unalterably good, that is certain. But imagine a world in which God were good, but not merciful. It wouldn't last long at all—perfect goodness would require justice, and we would all be given our just punishment for sin.

Yet a world where God was merciful, but not good would be a horrible place where sin would abound unchecked and unheeded. The perfect harmony of goodness and mercy are indeed ample reason to praise our God. He is good, and His perfect goodness requires justice, but aren't you glad that God is also merciful? 2 Corinthians 5:21 puts it this way:

"For He hath made Him to be sin for us, Who knew no sin, that we might be made the righteousness of God in Him."

The cross is the product of goodness combined with mercy. Romans 2:4 tells us that God's goodness leads us to repentance. As His goodness leads us there, His mercy makes a way for us to follow through, to have forgiveness of the sin of which we have repented.

Each day we live is a fresh opportunity to see God's goodness and mercy on display in our lives as we wholeheartedly trust and obey Him.

How has God shown His mercy and goodness to you today?

13

What He Can Do

"PONDER ANEW WHAT THE ALMIGHTY CAN DO"

G od is truly the Almighty. He has all power and is able to do all things. In our weakness and human limitations, we can all too easily become discouraged and feel that the difficulties of life are insurmountable. But we serve the Almighty God, and as the angel told Mary,

"For with God, nothing shall be impossible." Luke 1:37

What does that mean for you and me today? Simply this:

God is able.

He is stronger than our fiercest temptations, bigger than our most overwhelming problems, and infinitely loving. Whatever you may be facing today, God can handle it! Let's take a few moments to "ponder anew" what our Almighty God can do.

You may remember that earlier in this book we looked at Jeremiah 32, and Jeremiah's conversation with the Lord about the truth that there is nothing too hard for the Lord. But there are many other times God has shown His power.

Think of Abraham and Sarah, aged and childless, yet when God announced that the time had come for Him to give them the son He had promised, notice what He says in the face of Sarah's unbelief:

"Is any thing too hard for the Lord?"

Sometimes we don't look at life with the eyes of faith. Instead, we wrestle with our earthly thinking, almost afraid to believe that God is able to do what He has promised. But as the angel told Mary when she wondered at the physical impossibility of a virgin birth,

"For with God, nothing shall be impossible." (Luke 1:37)

What is there that seems "too hard," today?
Will you choose to trust the Almighty God with it?

14

Befriended by God

"IF WITH HIS LOVE HE BEFRIEND THEE."

"Henceforth I call you not servants; for the servant knoweth not what his lord doeth: but I have called you friends; for all things that I have heard of My Father I have made known unto you." John 15:15

Think of the majesty and holiness of our great God. He is so infinitely higher, wiser, stronger, and better than we are, and yet, He chooses to call us His *friends*. Let the contrast sink in, and inspire a sense of wonder—it is a truth well worth wondering at!

But with the sense of wonder comes a question: "How can this be?" The simple answer is that God, in His mercy has befriended us. Not only does He call all to salvation *(John 12:32)*, those who respond to that call in faith are brought into fellowship with Him as His friends.

James 2:23 gives us an illustration of how this works:

"And the scripture was fulfilled which saith, Abraham believed God, and it was imputed unto him for righteousness: and he was called the Friend of God."

Abraham believed, and was made righteous, and befriended by God. So too, you and I who have believed in Christ exchange our sin for His righteousness and are made friends of God.

But Jesus also said,

"Greater love hath no man than this, that a man lay down his life for his friends. Ye are My friends, if ye do whatsoever I command you." (John 15:13-14)

It was Christ's great love that moved Him to lay His life down for us. But what is all this about doing what He commands? I think Jesus' words from John 14:23 can help us understand this:

"If a man love Me, he will keep My words: and my Father will love him, and We will come unto him, and make Our abode with him."

Christlike love requires action, and just as God's love for us, His friends, led to sacrifice, so our love for our Divine Friend should motivate us to sacrificial obedience. Christ's example teaches us that true friendship does not balk at hard things, but embraces sacrifice. To keep ourselves in the love of God, as Jude 1:21 puts it, we must live each day knowing and rejoicing in His love for us--and then actively pouring that love out again in selfless obedience to the Holy Spirit's promptings.

Friend of God, how is your love? What sacrificial obedience is the Holy Spirit calling you to today?

15

When Tempests are Raging

PRAISE TO THE LORD, WHO, WHEN TEMPESTS THEIR WARFARE ARE WAGING, WHO, WHEN THE ELEMENTS MADLY AROUND THEE ARE RAGING,

A quick search of the word "tempests" in the Bible will confirm that such storms are not looked upon as a blessing. In fact, tempests are often used to describe or illustrate the wrath of God. But we sometimes experience storms even when we are in the will of God.

The disciples faced a tempest with Jesus right there in the boat with them.

"And when He was entered into a ship, His disciples followed Him. And behold, there arose a great tempest in the sea, insomuch that the ship was covered with the waves: but He was asleep." Matthew 8:23-24

Imagine being a disciple in that storm. You've followed Jesus Himself onto the boat in the first place, but suddenly, the winds and waves begin to rise.

Perhaps it was those disciples who were fishermen who were the first to notice the signs: a sharp breeze, a change in the air, or a small shifting of the pattern of waves on the surface of the water. I can imagine their distress as the storm grew and grew, to the point where the waves were crashing over the ship. In fact, the parallel account in Mark 4 tells us that the ship was actually full of water. No wonder they panicked!

And where was Jesus? Still asleep. You and I know the end of the story, but put yourself in their place. Would you be wondering how Jesus could be asleep in such a life-threatening situation? When they woke Jesus, they said,

"Lord, save us: we perish." (Matthew 8:25) Mark 4:38 gives us more detail: *"Master, carest Thou not that we perish?"*

Are you in a tempest today? Does it feel like you are frantically bailing water while the waves continue to fill your boat? Are you tempted to ask if God even cares?

Remember Jesus' words to the disciples that day: *"Why are ye fearful, O ye of little faith?"* Regardless of whether God rebukes your storm, or simply gives you grace to weather it, we can praise Him that He is present and in control—even when we think He is sleeping.

***How is the Holy Spirit calling you to trust
through your tempest today?***

16

Turning Fury to Peace

BIDDETH THEM CEASE, TURNETH THEIR FURY TO PEACE, WHIRLWINDS AND WATERS ASSUAGING.

"*What manner of Man is this, that even the winds and the sea obey Him!*" *(Matthew 8:27)*

The disciples were in a storm-filled boat, tossing violently in the tempest, and where was Jesus?

Sleeping peacefully in the boat.

His disciples woke Him, asking Him to save them, for without His help, they would certainly be drowned.

I don't get a sense of urgency from Jesus' recorded response to the disciples in any of the Gospel accounts. He rebukes their lack of faith, and then speaks to the wind and waves, which instantly become still.

We often smile at their wonder—after all, they were with *Jesus*, and they had even asked for His help! But how often do you and I do the same thing when overwhelmed by a tempest? We feel hopeless, and cry out to God, and then when the answer comes, we are filled with wonder at His power and mercy.

And yet, *we are with Jesus.* We can ask for His help, knowing He will give it. *(1 John 5:14; John 14:14)*

The disciples displayed a measure of faith when they asked Jesus to help them, but Jesus' rebuke reveals a lack of faith in the results. Perhaps they believed that He would try to help them, but doubted that He was able. Or perhaps they expected His help to come in some lesser form, like help with bailing water to keep the ship afloat.

Whatever they expected, the reality surpassed their wildest imaginations! We are sometimes like the disciples, asking for help, but not really expecting Him to, or else, expecting His help to come in a specific form. But God reminds us,

"For My thoughts are not your thoughts, neither are your ways My ways, saith the Lord. For as the heavens are higher than the earth, so are My ways higher than your ways, and My thoughts than your thoughts." (Isaiah 55:8-9)

Our God is worthy of praise, not just for His ability to calm tempests, but also for His wisdom in knowing how to build our faith. I am sure the disciples' faith was strengthened by Jesus' miracle, and we know they were amazed (and a little frightened) by His command over the wind and waves.

So, too, you and I need our faith strengthened. We need to experience those moments of awe and holy fear at the magnitude of God's power and mercy. Sometimes, like the disciples, all we need is faith enough to ask.

What is it that you need God's help with today?

17

When Sin is Abounding

PRAISE TO THE LORD, WHO, WHEN DARKNESS OF SIN IS ABOUNDING, WHO, WHEN THE GODLESS DO TRIUMPH, ALL VIRTUE CONFOUNDING,

"Help, Lord; for the godly man ceaseth; for the faithful fail from among the children of men." Psalm 12:1

Do you sometimes look around and wonder why God allows so much wickedness in the world? The prophet Jeremiah did, and took the matter up with God:

"Righteous art Thou, O Lord, when I plead with Thee: yet let me talk with Thee of Thy judgments: Wherefore doth the way of the wicked prosper? Wherefore are all they happy that deal very treacherously?" (Jeremiah 12:1)

God's answer, found later in that same chapter, reminds Jeremiah that He *will* bring judgment. You see, God is always just, but He sees the whole picture, and in His justice, leaves room for mercy, and time for the wicked to repent.

If you find yourself discouraged at the seeming prosperity of the wicked, remember that God's justice transcends the bounds of our understanding. Just as He delayed judgment on the nations of the land of Canaan, *"for the iniquity of the Amorites is not yet full." (Genesis 15:16),* So, too, He may be delaying judgment on a particular nation, people group, or individual until they have reached the furthest extent of His mercy.

So what do we do when faced with the reality of evil in this fallen world? Psalm 73 gives us an illustration of a God-ward response to the prosperity of the wicked. Discouraged and feeling that his own righteousness is almost in vain, the psalmist has a shift in perspective:

"Until I went into the sanctuary of God; then understood I their end." *(v.17)*

When we set our focus on the injustices and evil of our world, it can be easy to feel we are on the losing side. But that is simply not so! When faced with the prosperity and abundance of the wicked, we need to praise God for His longsuffering (1 Peter 3:20; 2 Peter 3:9) and His justice, remembering that He has already won the victory.

What discourages you about our wicked world?
How can you view it from the perspective of God's
mercy, longsuffering, and justice?

18

Sheddeth His Light

SHEDDETH HIS LIGHT, CHASETH THE HORRORS OF NIGHT

"This then is the message which we have heard of Him, and declare unto you, that God is light, and in Him is no darkness at all." (1 John 1:5)

This world can seem dark, indeed, but instead of letting the darkness drive us to despair, God wants us to live in His light.

"Ye are all the children of light, and the children of the day: we are not of the night, nor of the darkness." (1 Thessalonians 5:5)

The contrast between the darkness of this world and the perfect light of Christ is yet another reason for us to praise the Lord. In fact, it is part of our purpose as believers:

"But ye are a chosen generation, a royal priesthood, an holy nation, a peculiar people; that ye should shew forth the praises of Him who hath called you out of darkness into His marvellous light." (1 Peter 2:9)

When we go through our lives feeling dejected and defeated by the darkness of this word, we are not fulfilling our purpose. Likewise, if our lives are characterized by the world's darkness, we will not be bringing praise and glory to the God who rescued us from that darkness. We were saved *out* of the darkness, in order to shew forth His praises!

As 1 John 1:7 puts it, *"If we walk in the light, as He is in the light, we have fellowship one with another, and the blood of Jesus Christ His Son cleanseth us from all sin."*

Jesus Himself has commissioned us to be bright reflections of His light:

"Ye are the light of the world. A city that is set on an hill cannot be hid. Neither do men light a candle, and put it under a bushel, but on a candlestick; and it giveth light unto all that are in the house. Let your light so shine before men, that they may see your good works, and glorify your Father which is in heaven." (Matthew 5:14-16)

The darkness of this world is great, indeed, but we are to shine all the more brightly for the depth of the darkness, to spread the light of Christ to those still lost in the night.

Are you walking in the light of Christ today?
How does the Holy Spirit want your life to "shew forth the praises" of
God?

19

Surrounded by Mercy

SAINTS WITH HIS MERCY SURROUNDING.

Sometimes, God miraculously stills the tempests of our lives, but other times, He chooses to show his power by giving us grace as we weather them. Jesus said,

"These things have I spoken unto you, that in Me ye might have peace. In the world ye shall have tribulation: but be of good cheer; I have overcome the world." John 16:33

Jesus *has* overcome the world. Tribulations, though not at all pleasant, give us a chance to exercise our faith and grow closer to God as we yield ourselves to His mercy. 1 Peter 4:12-13 says,

"Beloved, think it not strange concerning the fiery trial which is to try you, as though some strange thing happened unto you: But rejoice, inasmuch as ye are partakers of Christ's sufferings; that, when His glory shall be revealed, ye may be glad also with exceeding joy."

Whatever trials and tribulations we may experience, we will never be out of reach of the mercy of God. In fact, God's mercy is the very reason we exist in the first place, and certainly the reason that we are forgiven. 1 Peter again says,

"Blessed be the God and Father of our Lord Jesus Christ, which according to His abundant mercy hath begotten us again unto a lively hope by the resurrection of Jesus Christ from the dead, to an inheritance incorruptible, and undefiled, and that fadeth not away, reserved in heaven for you" (1:3-4)

So, what are we to do when going through a time of trials and tribulations?

"Wherefore, let them that suffer according to the will of God commit the keeping of their souls to Him in well doing, as unto a faithful Creator." (1 Peter 4:19)

The only way to have the peace and joy of God while going through trials is to surrender ourselves and the trial to God, trusting Him to use it for our good and His glory. His mercy is still there, still being poured out over us in our trial—but it takes the eyes of faith to see it.

How is the Holy Spirit asking you to "commit the keeping" of your soul to Him in faith today?

20

All That is in Me

PRAISE TO THE LORD, O LET ALL THAT IS IN ME ADORE HIM!

The adoration of God is something we often tend to do on the surface. We go to church and sing a few songs about God on Sunday, and maybe listen to or sing along with some songs of praise to God throughout the week. But as the psalmist said, the worship and adoration of our God should be something we enter into with our whole heart, soul and mind.

After all, Jesus said, quoting from Deuteronomy 6:5,

"thou shalt love the Lord thy God with all thy heart, and with all thy soul, and with all thy mind, and with all thy strength: this is the first commandment." (Mark 12:30)

Old and New Testament agree (of course) that our love of God is to be all-encompassing. But so often, we hold back parts of our hearts, our souls, or our minds. We allow ourselves to cling to a secret bit of sin, or to be distracted by the "important" things of life.

But love—and therefore, worship—of God is meant to fill every part of our being. James 4:4 puts it bluntly:

"Ye adulterers and adulteresses, know ye not that the friendship of the world is enmity with God? Whosoever therefore will be a friend of the world is the enemy of God."

We are called to be wholly, faithfully devoted to God—to hold nothing back, but to put Him first in every area of life. You and I are truly to praise the Lord with *"all that is in me"*

What are you holding back today?
Take some time to ask the Holy Spirit to show you any parts of your heart, mind, soul or strength held back from loving God.

21

All that Hath Life and Breath

ALL THAT HATH LIFE AND BREATH, COME NOW WITH PRAISES BEFORE HIM;

"Let every thing that hath breath praise the Lord. Praise ye the Lord."
Psalm 150:6

The hymn writer echoes the words of the psalmist when he calls on "all that hath life and breath" to praise the Lord. This is actually another part of our purpose as Christians. Hebrews 3:13 tells us,

"But exhort one another daily, while it is called To day; lest any of you be hardened through the deceitfulness of sin."

The Greek word translated "exhort" here literally means to call near, or invite. Taking the context into consideration, this verse is telling us as believers that we are to call others near, or invite them to greater faith in Christ, so none of us succumb to *"an evil heart of unbelief, in departing from the living God."(v.12)*

When we are grumbling, complaining, or whining, we are speaking words of unbelief. Part of our purpose as Christians is to call others closer to Christ. We are to encourage each other to walk in faith, and one of the ways we can do that is to call each other to praise the Lord.

I am blessed with several friends who are faithful to point out the hand of God in any situation. This helps me to respond those situations in faith, instead of doubt. You and I have a powerful opportunity to help our fellow Christians to exercise their faith. And we can do this simply by being quick to praise the Lord.

Notice that the psalmist is not alone in Psalm 122:1

"I was glad when they said unto me, Let us go into the house of the Lord."

May our hearts and words of praise inspire contagious joy and point others to faith-filled praise of our most praiseworthy God!

Do you have a heart of praise? How does God desire to use you to "exhort" other Christians today?

22

Forever Adoring

LET THE AMEN SOUND FROM HIS PEOPLE AGAIN, GLADLY FOR AYE WE ADORE HIM.

Have you ever thought about the fact that praise is not just something we do here on earth? The expression "for aye" used by the hymnwriter means forever, or eternally. Psalm 86:12 says,

"I will praise Thee, O Lord my God, with all my heart: and I will glorify Thy name for evermore."

For the Christian, this isn't just an expression: we are given the privilege of eternity with the Lord! Paul, writing about the rapture of the believers in 1 Thessalonians 4:17 says,

"Then we which are alive and remain shall be caught up together with them in the clouds, to meet the Lord in the air: and so shall we ever be with the Lord."

And for those of us who die before the return of Christ, we have the same promise of eternity with the Lord. Jesus Himself told His disciples (and recorded it for us as well),

"In my Father's house are many mansions: if it were not so, I would have told you. I go to prepare a place for you. And if I go and prepare a place for you, I will come again, and receive you unto Myself; that where I am there ye may be also." John 14:2-3

Our adoration of God during our earthly lives is but a fleeting glimmer in comparison with the never ending light of eternity.

"So we Thy people and sheep of Thy pasture will give Thee thanks for ever: we will shew forth Thy praise to all generations." Psalm 79:13

What about an eternity of praising God fills your heart with joy? Praise Him for it now!

www.ingramcontent.com/pod-product-compliance
Lightning Source LLC
Chambersburg PA
CBHW060355130626
46553CB00003B/1242